WARNING

DANGER, KEEP OUT, DO NOT ENTER, NO
HUNTING, PRIVATE PROPETY,
BEWARE OF MEN WITH BIG GENITALS.
Men have fought over food, water, women, and gold
since the beginning of time. This battle to be king of the
mountain never ends.

With all the important information men have
painstakingly inscribed on rocks, painted on walls and
scribbled on paper; they still feel the need to
exaggerate.

I've chosen these ancient petroglyphs for the cover and
theme of this book.

These exaggerations are much older and greater than
mine.

I suffer from the curse of having a 3rd opinion and 3rd
opinions are not popular.

YOU'VE BEEN WARNED

Outlaw Tales of the Superstition Mountains

Arlin Troutt

Outlaw Tales of the Superstition Mountains

Front cover photograph by Patrick Lange
Cover design by Guy Corp, www.GrafixCorp.com

STAIRWAY≡PRESS

STAIRWAY PRESS—APACHE JUNCTION

www.stairwaypress.com
1000 West Apache Trail, Suite 126
Apache Junction, AZ 85120 USA

FOREWORD

IN 1994, I was a relatively new editor at *High Times* magazine. I had written several stories, but hadn't really encountered the true movers and shakers who were pushing for marijuana legalization.

That all changed when I flew to Arizona to cover the formation of the Hemp Industries Association.

The people who gathered in that hotel conference room in Paradise Valley weren't just entrepreneurs trying to create a market for hemp products. They were activists, environmentalists, legal minds and quite a few outlaws. I use the term "outlaw" in the best sense of the word: a person excluded from the benefit or protection of the law, or an unconventional or rebellious individual. There were plenty of those in attendance.

This is where I met Arlin "Junior" Troutt. He and his colleagues had been smuggling thousands of pounds of Mexican marijuana into the U.S. since the early 1970s. Some had thrived while others had been in prison and some still were. The federal government was waging a frenzied campaign to stamp out marijuana, using the War on Drugs to eradicate the plant and punish those who engaged in illegal commerce. Law enforcement had intensified and the stakes were much higher. Still, many smugglers continued their work, despite the steep penalties that awaited them if they were apprehended.

Arlin was one of them.

Funding a legal hemp business with ill-gotten pot money offered an opportunity to deliver a backhand smack to the Feds. Arlin and his wife Cathy founded U.S. Hemp in 1991 offering an array of products. They were activists as well. Arlin was one of the leaders of protests at the 1993 National Summit on U.S. Drug Policy in San Antonio, TX. He and others set up cannabis information tables and gave the media hard facts about industrial hemp and marijuana. But his activism came with a price. Law enforcement was well aware of his history and his outspokenness made him a target.

In 1996, he was sentenced to more than eight years in prison after being found guilty of conspiring to possess more than 100 pounds of marijuana. But even behind bars, he would not go away. He ran for vice-president in 1996 as the running mate of Dennis Peron, the presidential candidate of the Grass Roots Party.

I've now known Arlin for nearly 30 years. He has a remarkably sunny personality, is full of stories and regrets nothing. He's also a musician extraordinaire, an excellent guitarist and vocalist. And he's a devoted family man with six kids and, so far, four grandchildren.

My 25-year career with *High Times* came to an end in 2017, but I learned more about cannabis and the meaning of liberty from outlaws than from any of the many other people I covered.

When Arlin was sentenced in 1996, here's what he had to say:

> *Fear and ignorance guided by greed and blind ambition created the prohibition of hemp. I am morally and intellectually compelled to resist these forces. When the American people find out what hemp is and why it's really illegal, may they deal with this government as harshly as it has dealt with me.*

If that's what an "outlaw" says, I want to be one.

—Malcolm MacKinnon

Malcolm MacKinnon is a photojournalist who has covered the cannabis scene since 1991. He is the former editor-in-chief of *High Times* magazine.

MalcolmMacKinnon.com

CHAPTER ONE—ROCKS AND WATER

THE SUPERSTITION MOUNTAINS tower over a hot harsh land of fire, flood, earthquake, and drought. With no horses or wheels, an ancient and advanced culture built large cities hundreds of years ago. They built roads and networks of canals that still carry water across this desert today. But what happened to these horseless and wheelless natives? Why did they simply disappear leaving only ruins, graves and broken pottery fading in the sun with my shuffleboard court?

The Indians left, the Spaniards left, the movie stars left. They left me to guard this vacant paradise with a deed to an unwanted land that could never be resold or returned to non-Caucasians.

J'Trene Troutt, Freddie Lee Troutt, Hieroglyphic Springs, in the Superstition Mountains

Long before I came to this mountain, non-Caucasians scratched stories on flat rock surfaces around my old ranch house. Among other things, the petroglyphs warn us of perilous journeys into our rocky, dry, and wet canyons.

These petroglyphs also map and deed ownership of water and ancient hunting trails. I'll always wonder why the people who hunted the gold, dug the graves, broke the clay pots, made movies and played shuffleboard left this Superstition Mountain paradise to me.

Water is the lifeline that maps the migration of all humanity. According to the U.S. Geological Service, based on tree growth, 1942-1964 was the most severe drought for Arizona in 350 years. Toward the end of the first great drought, the Spaniards came with horses and wheels hunting for gold, silver, and slaves around 1540. The mission required water and they didn't stay long.

Rock writings exaggerate but they don't lie about the danger. The similarity between the rock writings in the Superstition Mountains and the mountainous desert lands around the world are amazing.

The rocks on this ridge held maps of the mountains and trails across this desert. The rocks told stories of the "water tank wars" over the very hill my old ranch house sets on. There are still fragments of a rock writing here that once told the story of a massacre of Spaniards and mules by natives.

After the Indian wars the battle to protect non-Caucasian history came. But it was a losing battle. The rock stories by my house and across this desert were broken into pieces, strewn, and hauled off for souvenirs. Tourists picked up pottery pieces by the bags and buckets off these sacred burial grounds.

In 1964, the Superstition Wilderness was established to protect the mountain and its history. However, there was nothing in place to protect Gold Canyon from the treasure hunters and wildcat land developers who followed.

CHAPTER TWO—NAVAJO MEDICINE MAN

THE OLD DIRT road from highway 60 to the ridge was littered in places with broken pottery from a much earlier

time. Some chards were plain and utilitarian, others ornately painted.

It was common to find a broken arrowhead or robbed Indian grave on the side of a hill. Southwestern Indians drill holes in their burial pots and then break pots into pieces above the graves.

That's one way to tell if old Indian pottery is stolen from a grave. Burial

4

pots will have a small finger size hole in a lower part or bottom of the pot. Grave robbers used to sell them on the table and under the table at the Phoenix Park and Swap.

Grave robbing is still a popular and disgusting pass time with serious karmic consequences.

Construction of the Gold Canyon Country Club and the housing developments on Kings ranch were built on ground sacred to the Native Americans. Artifacts from ancient ceremonies and burials were dug up, collected, or quietly plowed, broken and buried by bulldozers.

You can't complain about the destruction of artifacts without bringing attention to their location and yourself. There is a silent war to protect these treasures.

Tom Kollenborn (our local and sadly deceased historian) translated an old Indian name for the Superstitions as Crooked Top Mountain.

Raymond Jim (Jimmy) was a Navajo medicine man and close friend until the day he died (on the solstice ironically). We spent a great deal of time together and I was with him the morning before he held his last sweat lodge in Safford Federal Prison.

Jimmy and other old Arizona natives told me stories about this area being used for large gatherings and burial

5

ceremonies. Indian tribes as far away as Canada and Central America gathered here. I've heard several people describe the Superstition Mountains as an ancient Indian cemetery called: "We Never Go There."

CHAPTER THREE—ENTRANCE TO THE UNDERWORLD

NATIVE AMERICANS FAR and near believed the entrance to the underworld was in the Superstition Mountains.

This underworld myth may have formed around the mouth of a cave wide enough for 7 braves to ride 7 horses side by side.

This story would have come after the Spaniards brought horses, but earthquakes also came after the Spaniards. The Jesuits abruptly left after the loss of the Spanish Armada (1588) in their war with the British. They may have caved in the east side of Hog Canyon to deeply bury this cave entrance and the gold.

They would have returned with an army to build a city out of the rubble of rock and recover the gold. Be it Jesuits or earthquakes, something big happened in Hog canyon.

In 1887 there was a major earthquake in the Superstition Mountains centered around Weaver's Needle. The National Park Service considers this terrain in the Tonto National Forest the most unstable and dangerous of all our U.S. National Parks.

The east side of Hog Canyon on the southeast side of Flat Iron in the Superstitions may be where all the Spanish gold is deeply buried; stashed by Jesuits or lost in an earthquake.

I've looked at maps and listened to the lost Dutchman goldmine theories for 50 years. I've visited the camps and drank with many of the modern-day treasure hunters. Con Artists like Ron Eagle were selling maps to the lost Dutchman's gold mine to drunken tourists long before I arrived. See Tom Kollenborn's Chronicles: Eagle of the Superstition Mountain.[1]

This mystery of the missing cave and lost Spanish gold in the Superstitions has never been solved and this story has never been told.

---

[1]

http://superstitionmountaintomkollenborn.blogspot.com/2011/05/eagle-of-superstition-mountain.html

CHAPTER FOUR—THE BRIGHTEST STAR IN THE SKY

THE SUPERSTITION MOUNTAINS are a beautiful place to bury something precious.

I've spent a lot of peaceful time by my sister's grave at Top of the World. Mary Lynn was buried in a purple hemp dress, she loved kids, cannabis, pinata parties and purple was her favorite color.

Nothing can outshine the real stars in this desert sky on a dark moonless night and Mary Lynn is the brightest star in the sky.

Jimmy was with me when she died. The Navajo understanding of death is beautiful. I was grateful to have him with me through that great grief. I still water sis's pine tree and sprinkle peridot on her grave when I visit the Top of the World. I still think of Jimmy often.

CHAPTER FIVE—APACHELAND MOVIE RANCH

I'M NOT SURE when it dawned on me that the old cowboy movies my sister and I watched together as kids were filmed here in Gold Canyon. Apacheland Movie Ranch is where the cowboy movies and stars I watched on TV as a boy out glittered the stars.

I wonder if there is a human mind on Earth that is untouched by Hollywood. Our minds were filled with stories about Indian raids, highway bandits, lost gold mines, and bible thumping, claim-jumping land swindlers.

These outlaw stories were and still are hugely popular across the globe.

Ronald Reagan hosted a long running TV show called "Death Valley Days." Old maps show my land setting on the "water tank" Those 20 mule team ore wagons featured in his shows really stopped at the bottom of this hill for water in the old days.

Reagan later used his facial recognition and popularity from grade B movies and TV to become Governor of California and President of the United States.

Weekly episodes of Wyatt Earp, Have Gun Will Travel, The Rifleman, Rawhide, The Virginian and Wanted Dead or Alive are still being watched and shaping minds all over the world.

Movie stars like Elvis Presley, Steve McQueen and many other celebrities left their mark on humanity with these old movies.

They left their handprints and signatures inscribed on concrete slabs at Apacheland movie ranch. Those were broken in pieces and taken like the rock writings and burial pots.

The view from the house was especially spectacular on the rainy days. The movie ranch ruins looked mysterious in the morning fog, and I drove down for a closer look.

The roof had burned off, but tall cinderblock walls were partially standing. There was a black, badly beaten grand piano setting in the roofless rubble.

It was surreal or "trippy." I imagined the hustle and bustle of producing the movies and TV shows I had intermingled with reality and loved as a child.

I idealized these mountains and movie stars captured on film for all eternity in this sacred land.

Cowboy movies left me and the rest of the world with a fantastic view of reality that still shapes our lives and society today.

I made up my own Episode of Death Valley Days. This is a short story about a barber named Ernie and his dumb brother Joe that came to Arizona from New York City. They came to the old wild west to make their fortune scalping Indians in the Superstition Mountains. They had only managed to get a couple of scalps before they rested for the night. Joe awoke the next morning surrounded by Apache Indians. He quietly whispered: *"Wake up, Ernie, we're rich."*

CHAPTER SIX—TONTO

THE TONTO NATIONAL Forest that encompasses the Superstition Mountains is in the Tonto Basin. This area is so rugged Spaniards called these inhabitants of mixed tribes Tonto Apache. The Spaniards and even surrounding tribes considered these inhabitants dumb or foolish to live in such a rugged and punishing place.

The Apache were outlaws and the people who came to the Superstition Mountains prepared and expected to live outside of the law. Lead bullets probably outweighed all the gold prospectors found.

I did not realize when my sister and I went to the movies or watched Television we were being programmed and scripted into acting out the part of modern-day outlaws.

Recite this line in Tonto's voice:

Passing screech of hawk echoing off mountain speaks to whispering wind caught in cactus.

Sis and I watched the Lone Ranger and Tonto on TV when we were kids. Later I saw the same shows dubbed in Spanish south of the border, but they changed Tonto's name to Toro which means a bull in English. Tonto means stupid in Spanish and Mexico has a lot of Indians. So, south of the border it was the Lone Ranger and Toro on TV. And when you think about it: why did Tonto keep going into town for supplies while the Lone Ranger hid out at camp? Where did the money come from?

The Lone Ranger wore a black mask on his face, skin tight tights, rode a snow-white horse, with a silver saddle and loaded his gun with silver bullets. The Lone Ranger was the old west version of a Hollywood pimp. I knew a few of them.

Some scenes from these old movies are controversial, socially awkward and hard to watch today. They clearly contain evidence of systemic racial and gender prejudice and disparity. But ironically, they also contain overt moral messages about honesty, law and order, and the mistreatment of horses, dogs, white women, Mexicans and Indians (in that order).

Overall, these old western movies had a great deal to do with who we are today collectively and individually. We all have a little Hollywood cowboy and cowgirl in us.

The mixed messages are mind boggling. The fine line between the good guy and the bad guy got blurry on black and white TV.

Finance, floods, and fires finally finished off Apacheland but the movies, stories and tales of the Superstition Mountains still interest the world.

It's easy to imagine that a lot of fortunes changed hands and a lot of serious crimes were never reported or resolved in the Superstition Mountains.

Hollywood has brought the world's attention to this mountain and these old outlaw stories. But the movie studio burned, and the gold diggers left. And its time to tell the Outlaw Tales of Latter-Day Crimes.

Where does a good story start and when does it end? My stories start in the moonshining hollers north of Nashville and end in the Superstition Mountains someday, but not today.

CHAPTER SEVEN—THE MASON/DIXON LINE

MY BIRTH CAME in January of 1950 in Layfette, Tennessee (pronounced Lafet). My sister was born in Lafayette, Indiana (pronounced La Fay Yet) in August of 1951. Both Northern and Southern pronunciations are still used in these Yankee and Rebel towns separated by the great state of Kentucky.

I was the first baby in my family delivered in a hospital. Mom and I were the first in our family to ever ride in an ambulance. She said my birth drew a big crowd of family and friends at the hospital. We were both delivered back to the farm in the hospital ambulance for a spectacular show of Macon county modernization. That was my first performance.

17

My Creek Indian and Scottish ancestors lived in the woods of the high hills along the creek banks. These areas were less populated than the larger lowland rivers.

Every 2nd Wednesday my pa would sometimes take my excited cousin and I to Indian trade day in Lafayette. There were no Indians, or blacks, mostly old white men swapping knives and exaggerating about the size of fish, intelligence of mules and quality of tobacco crops.

The first time I ever saw any black people was on the dirt road in front of Pa Mc's house.

It was a new fancy car full of people. They all had dark skin and smiled and waved when they passed. I ran to the barn where Pa was putting new horseshoes on Big Bob. I explained what I saw, and he smiled and said: that's the Alexanders coming home for Thanksgiving.

Mr. Jim and Miss Minny Alexander's farm was a goat's ride away and my home away from home. Their farmhouse and barns were gigantic. I did not know the difference in the slave farms and small farms then.

After the civil war many slaves took the family names of their owners. But some of these families had lived with each other for generations and loved each other.

This had a lot to do with the music in those hills. Real country music is a Scottish, Indian, African cocktail they call Bluegrass.

Lafayette, Tennessee was in the war zone "south" of the Mason/Dixon line. This line divided the north from the south in the American Civil War. Macon county was in the poorer northern part of Tennessee. South part of Tennessee had more slave owners that sided with the Confederate Rebels. My family fought on both sides in the Civil War. Pa told me stories about the Dupont family in Castalian Springs selling gunpowder to both sides.

The Macon County Seat was established in Lafayette in 1842. There have been three courthouse fires in Lafayette since 1934. This was common all through the south after the civil war. They were burning land deeds and embarrassing interracial marriage and birth certificates.

Though this unusually bloody and brutal war officially ended in 1864 it is still being fought in many ways even today.

Removal of Confederate hero statues erected long after the end of the Civil War is a good example of the deep and lasting division this war left behind.

American land grants to early settlers and Indians were

often given for war service. These lands were not all taken from the native Tennessee tribes. My ancestors were exempt from the Trail of Tears march to Oklahoma. Ironically our Native American land grants came from service to the British during the

20

Revolutionary War of 1776. These British land grants had more legal standing than later land grants and statues of Confederate war heroes.

CHAPTER EIGHT— FROM THE HILLS OF TENNESSEE

MY FIRST MEMORIES are of my family's tobacco farms in Macon County, the poorest and most rural county in Tennessee, I was told. We plowed our fields with horses and cleared the rocky pastures by hand. The men in my family grew and smoked their own tobacco. They made moonshine and drank it behind the barn in moderation and secrecy before I came. My great grandmother (Granny Mc) still called the shots and set the rules of the house (No Alcohol).

We all smoked the ham and bacon in Macon. The women cooked and canned the fruits and vegetables. We farmed the fields, hunted and gathered in the woods. We collected honey and maple syrup and made our own molasses, medicine, soap, cookies, and some of our clothes.

McDole family farm outside of Westmoreland, Tennessee. It has been restored by Mike McDole. Every detail in this drawing stirs memories and makes me long for those simpler times, smoked ham, buttered biscuits and black berry jam or jelly for breakfast.

We bathed in the waterhole where Easley and Trammel Creek forked with a bar of lye soap. After supper I sang hymns with my family on Pa Mc's front porch till dark. I spent a great deal of time singing in the amen corner at church with Pa Duffy and my first cousin Freddie Lee Spears.

CHAPTER NINE— READIN, RIGHTIN AND ROUTE 31 NORTH

I **WAS BORN** the same year the remote control for televisions was invented. We didn't have a TV or running water in our house then. We walked to the spring up the hill for buckets of sweet water, we had an outhouse. Kids were responsible for inventing their own entertainment.

Mom and Dad moved around a lot during my childhood. There were a lot of happy hellos and sad goodbyes. Sis and I spent a lot of time watching TV and being the new kids in class.

We migrated and commuted back and forth from Tennessee to Indiana on an old deadly two-lane highway: U.S.

Route 31. The weekend ride between Indiana to Tennessee on a Friday night was riddled with the drunken carnage of the Radio Cowboys. Dad was a Truck Driven Radio Cowboy. Whiskey and gas were cheap back then and still deadly when mixed. We were lucky, others weren't. Dad's head was seriously injured in a car accident while he was in the Army, and someone died. He never got over that and we all paid an emotional price with him.

The safest and happiest times were on my great-grandfather's tobacco farm with my Pa and Granny. Most of my summers were spent farming tobacco, fiddling in the fields, and fishing in the creeks.

Cowboys, kids and new schools can be rough. I was teased and bullied in Indianapolis by white kids because of my slow hillbilly ways. I had to fight black kids to and from school because of my white southern drawl.

Bruised, and bullied for being a hick in Indiana; Teased in Tennessee for talking like a Yankee: I blame Ma and Pa Kettle, the Beverly Hillbillies and Hollywood for the prejudice and injustices I suffered as a child.

However, I became good at doing impressions of movie stars (that no one remembers now). I got good at telling jokes to break the tough guy tension and playing guitar and singing silly songs to impress the girls.

That didn't always work. After the church, a child quartet and a knife fight with 2 schoolyard bullies in Tennessee I ended up back in Indianapolis again.

These bearded farm boys were much older and bigger

but, I was the only one that had a knife. It was clear from early years that I was a black sheep in a spotted flock on both sides of the Mason/Dixon line.

CHAPTER TEN— PA DUFFY AND THE COPPERHEAD

PA DUFFY WAS the most influential man in my life, and I suspect Freddie Lee feels the same. He was a 32-degree Master Freemason. He taught me about hounds, horses, hunting, the value of truth and honesty and the hardness of hickory.

He owned a 410 shotgun and a 22 single shot

27

rifle for hunting. He was a highly skilled and humane killer. He carried a small yellow handled case knife that he used to peal me an apple or skin a squirrel.

I watched him use that knife to pin a copperhead to the ground after it bit him. He sent me running for help; my first emergency.

Copperhead and water moccasin snakes around our creeks and springs looked similar. But the copperhead has a blunt tail. The water moccasin has a long thin tail, and the inside of their mouth is white when they hiss and show their fangs. The water moccasin will try to warn you the copperhead won't bother. The cotton mouth can be more dangerous and deadly. We had to retrieve the snake that bit my Pa and take it back to Dr. Carter because the antivenoms were different. That created a damaging delay.

My little Rat Terrier, Leroy took a lot of copperhead bites hunting through the weeds and woods in front of me. He would go to the creek and eat grass for 3 days and was back on the hunt. But the copperhead bite was bad for Pa and he was never the same nor was I.

I was biblically terrified of snakes before I saw my Pa get bit. I will always remember how fast it happened, then how calmly and methodically he cut and pulled his shoelaces for the torniquet, pinned the snakes head to the ground with his knife and calmly sent me for help.

I was anything but calm, but I was never afraid of snakes after that. They are not magical, mad or mean. They just require some space and respect.

CHAPTER ELEVEN—THE BOMB

FREDDIE LEE AND I grew up together like brothers on the farm with my sister Lynne and cousins Karen and Martha. My mom breast fed me, my sister Lynne and my cousins Freddie Lee, and Karen Ann. (God Bless and May You Rest in Peace Karen).

I never knew Pa Duffy wasn't my real grandfather until I was 12 years old. Freddie Lee's sister Karen got mad at me and dropped the devastating "he ain't your Pa" bomb. Seems I was the only one that didn't know. I had never even thought about it. I never felt distance or a difference in his love for me.

But that may explain why he had a little more time and tolerance for my eccentric ways. He did not spank me often but I'm grateful for every ass whooping I got from him.

I wanted to put my shoe in every step he made and learn everything he knew. I learned a great deal from Pa Duffy.

Freddie Lee and I watched the roosters fight secretly behind the barn on Saturday and sang in church on Sunday. Pa sang in a professional gospel quartet, and Freddie and I toured the Tennessee churches with him and sang in a child quartet.

Pa disliked gambling and pistols, he never owned one and used to say: Pistols are only made for killing men. He also said this to me after my first knife fight: The bigger the knife, the smaller the man.

Those words cut deeper than a knife will go.

Ambidexterity is a great advantage for braiding rope,

hoeing tobacco, and other farm boy chores. I favored my left hand with a fork, spoon and tobacco knife but hunted with right-handed bows and rifles. I shot pistols with my left hand.

Pa bought my first shotgun when I turned 11. He carefully picked a particular Stevens single shot 410 gage shotgun out of the Sears Roebuck catalog. He carved my initials in the stock. I had to stop, think, and push the safety off with my thumb before it would shoot one shell. That made me think twice about pulling the trigger and hitting the target. Safety always came first with Pa.

I loved my Pa Duffy, that farm, the music, magic, blackberry jelly and Jesus. I knew little else then and I still love them all now.

CHAPTER TWELVE— OUTLAW MUSIC

THE WORD HOLLER (to yell) comes from the word hollow which means empty or a small valley. Hollows are small enough to yell across. You call the cows from across the holler. My granny would holler for us when it was time for dinner and supper.

33

So, to yell across a hollow is to holler across a holler. In Tennessee if you can holler you can sing in church.

Pa Duffy started teaching Freddie Lee and me to harmonize and read music before words. You don't have to know how to read a book to read music. But reading music is different than dreaming music, and I've always been more of a dreamer than a reader.

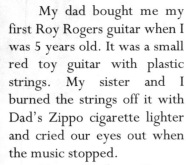

My dad bought me my first Roy Rogers guitar when I was 5 years old. It was a small red toy guitar with plastic strings. My sister and I burned the strings off it with Dad's Zippo cigarette lighter and cried our eyes out when the music stopped.

My Uncle Eugene (Freddie's dad) bought me my first real guitar when I was 9 years old (Regal F-hole arch top and back). It looked just like Roy's Gibson, but the strings were high off the fretboard and it was hard to chord.

I had been playing Uncle Eugene's 1952 Fender Telecaster since I was 6 years old.

He asked me if I wanted the strings reversed on the Regal because I favored my left hand.

I told him to leave it the way it was.

Jimmy Hendrix and many fine guitar players string their instrument in reverse and strum or pick the guitar with their left hand. They form the chords and play the melodies with the right hand.

The melodies that come out of my head show up in my left hand and my right hand just shoves them out the door.

Playing a guitar is like hunting with a rifle not shooting a pistol.

You aim a guitar at your prey with your left hand and pull the trigger with your right. Remember to smile.

Freddie and I could and would ride anything that had legs and play anything that had strings.

Freddie grew up and went on tour with David Allen Coe and the Tennessee Hat Band.

He climbed to the top of the outlaw music charts. I dug a hole and buried myself into the Vietnam anti-war underground.

But we always managed to find each other when it mattered. He loved fine wine, women, marijuana, money and bluegrass. He's one of my rowdy friends that settled down.

The songs Freddie has written, and albums recorded with David Allen Coe and other great artists says a lot about him and the Tennessee hills we came from. Freddie still plays with his old band buddies professionally, but I have to go to Texas to hear them.

We laughed, played and gambled from Nashville to Guadalajara and hid out in North Texas, Willie Nelson's golf course and the Superstition Mountains.

The stories of our adventures have never been told and haven't really ended. Musicians don't die until they stop making music and they don't stop making music until they die.

CHAPTER THIRTEEN—KILLER BEES, RUSSIAN BOMBS AND BULLIES

SCHOOLS CHANGED, BUT the bullying and bombs were similar. Every Friday morning air raid warning sirens screamed across Nashville and Indianapolis. My sister and I hid under our school desks in some sort of ritualistic rehearsal to survive Russian bombs and impending destruction.

Sis, our friends, and our entire generation of post WWII baby boomers were programed to live like there was no tomorrow. Everyone was in a hurry to go to war, get married, divorced and die, and everything was made of plastic.

Americans had an insatiable appetite for high-speed travel, handheld weapons of mass destruction, booze, drugs, taboo sex. This lust for instant gratification became part of the culture.

America was waiting for killer bees and Russian bombs, but it turned out to be the Beatles and Rolling Stones (bugs and rocks).

CHAPTER FOURTEEN—BOYS IN THE BAND

MY FIRST BAND (the Surfing Birds Combo) was formed right before the British rock invasion.

The Beatles were murdering old time Rock and Roll in the East. The Cream and Kinks were killing the Beach Boys on the West Coast. Fashion, language, sex, drugs, music, and the world were changing, my voice was changing. I was changing and puberty beat the hell out of me.

Everyone in the band was at least 3 years older and in high school. Their parents could afford musical instruments and lessons.

We all had a burning desire to be noticed, if not loved,

and worshiped in school. This was the earliest gustation period of the "garage band" and first birth pains of punk rock.

I wrote the chord charts for the songs and tried to teach my students how to sing church harmony. I taught Phil his rhythm guitar parts and Greg the bass guitar parts from scratch. Greg was a natural, Phil wasn't. We kept his volume on low.

Phil was jealous and always climbing on something to upstage me when we performed but he was intertaining. We played the popular rock and surf tunes of the day that did not require more than 3 chords.

Phil Bruce, Bill Quick, Arlin Troutt, Bob McCowen, Greg Brower and Frank Holland

CHAPTER FIFTEEN—CATHOLICS

FRANK HOLLAND WAS one of the most unique drummers I ever played with. Frank was so handsome our moms ogled him, and he left the girls speechless and giggling.

I spent a great deal of time at the Holland family's house and had a speechless crush on Frank's younger sister Jennie.

They were the first Catholic family I ever knew (Frank, Jennie, Joe, John, Mark). The Hollands always had an extra seat and plate at the table.

We were all seated for dinner—Baptists called it supper without the wine.

On one occasion we all noticed that Frank's plate was turned upside down. His mom had found his stash of Trojan rubbers in his top dresser drawer. I know what you're thinking: who hides things from their mother there?

I never said Frank was smart, I said he was a good drummer and I'll add: he was like a big brother to me. Rest in Peace Frank.

The look on Frank senior's face when Frank turned his plate over will stay with me forever. There was no screaming or drumstick drama. There was just this unusually long silence, and you could feel heat radiating from Mrs. Holland's mashed potatoes.

Frank calmly pocketed the prophylactics and filled his plate. The silence was replaced by the sounds of supper.

To this day, this was one of the most loving, caring and welcoming families I ever knew.

CHAPTER SIXTEEN—THE BOMB SHELTER

IRONICALLY, THE SURFING Birds had never seen a surfboard and I had an unnatural hillbilly fear of big fish and deep water. We can dive deeper into this phobia later if you promise not to laugh.

We had changed our name to the Chancellors by the time Greg Brower had arrived. The name was stolen off a 45 RPM by Chancellor Records.

We continued to get better and become popular around Indianapolis and the surrounding towns.

Greg Brower's family was also a loving, caring family. I spent a great deal of time at Greg's house teaching him to play the bass. I spent a few nights sleeping on their pool table. They were the only family I knew that had a pool table, a soda fountain in their basement and a gigantic place to rehearse the band. Underneath the basement they had a Russian cold war bomb shelter.

Greg's sisters were sweet, lovely, and wonderful friends. They were like sisters to me. The bomb shelter is where they went to smoke a puff or steal and innocent kiss. I still think about what would have happened in the case of a real air raid. Russian bombs that were never dropped stole a great deal of freedom from Americans. When will that nightmare end.

Greg's dad bought new professional Gibson amps for the band. I got a Gibson Firebird guitar to play, Greg got a matching Gibson Thunderbird bass.

The band sounded great but that Firebird was awkward, heavy and uncomfortable to play, standing or sitting. That's when Gibson started getting gimmicky.

Greg's dad financed the Chancellor's first 45 RPM titled Colt 45 (named after a fortified beer that came out in 1963). Unfortunately, I was not on that first vinyl record.

This hot surfer guitar player moved to Fort Harrison, Indiana from California and enrolled at Lawrence Central High.

His dad was a colonel in the U.S. Army. Tex was the same age as the other guys in the band and he was the American dream of the day. He was a terrific athlete, he had super sandy blond hair, blue eyes, a surfboard and a Fender guitar. Frank, Phil and Greg, voted me out of my own band for Tex. Bill Quick (sax) refused. That's democracy in action.

Bill left the band and they picked up my best friend Phil Ray to play the piano.

To make things even worse, my girlfriend and love of my life dumped me for my best friend Phil. I had lots of girlfriends and best friends after that.

And to make all of that even worse, Tex was a genuinely nice guy. But that did not matter. I hated him, my ex-girlfriend and my older backstabbing buddies that gave me my first lesson in abject betrayal. After all, it was Junior Troutt that transformed the Surfing Birds into the worshiped waveless surfers they had become.

Arlin Troutt

CHAPTER SEVENTEEN—SHELL SHOCK

TEX ENLISTED IN the Army before I graduated from high school, and I heard he was killed in Vietnam. I still think about him and how good he was on the guitar. I finally forgave him for being handsome and good at everything he did.

But I have never been able to forgive the government for Vietnam. I still hate that war because it took the absolute best my generation had to offer the world and deeply divided this nation.

Many friends came back from Vietnam in body bags and strait jackets. The dead are named in hieroglyphs etched on cold marble monuments.

The only thing that was working to help return some of these shell-shocked soldiers to their friends and family was marijuana. I've been practicing medicine without a license ever since. Marijuana is still the number one alternative and treatment for violent behavior, alcoholism, tobacco abuse, drug addiction and every level of stress society has to offer.

The nutritional value of the hemp seed alone makes the 1937 Prohibition of Marijuana a crime against humanity.

March of 1961 President John F. Kennedy signed the United Nations Single Treaty.

This made the cultivation of hemp illegal in Africa, the United States and other nations that commercially farmed hemp.

The Africans lost their number one food, fuel, fiber, and medicine crop. Then they lost their topsoil. Millions starved and died in desperate tribal wars for food, water and land.

This was no different than killing the buffalo to starve the Indians. The exploitation of human weakness in not what makes humans humane.

We are still suffering casualties from the post traumatic shock of these many different wars.

It's hard to tally the real damage of this U.S. Drug War. This war has raged in our streets for over 50 years with no end in sight. I believe I've made my feelings clear on this subject. Let's move on.

CHAPTER EIGHTEEN—FROM THE GROUND UP

I WAS RUNNING with an older crowd but still a little young to understand why the older girls were interested in me. Parading around under colored lights in pegged pants is like dragging a fishing lure behind your boat; Ya never know what you might unintentionally snag.

I had a mild form of shell shock or Post Traumatic Stress Disorder after the Chancellors broke my heart and took my Firebird guitar and girlfriend.

This is where puppy love and hippie Karma collide.

Bruce Morford in front, Steve Grimes, Jim Inman, Arlin Troutt and Bob Morford

Surf music and old-time rock and roll were the first casualties in the British invasion and music wars that ensued.

You could buy a used Fender or Les Paul guitar for $25 in a pawn shop. Every kid in America wanted an imported Rickenbacker guitar or Hofner bass shaped like a fiddle for Christmas.

I quickly accepted the reality of my great loss of time and prestige with my old band. Great losses in life are met with mixed emotions and reactions. My reaction was to start from scratch and change everything from the ground up to avoid loss and future disappointment. Never have an emotional attachment to a name or place. Now remind yourself I said this later.

I recruited upcoming musicians from the 8th grade at Belzer Junior High, revised the repertoire and named the band Junior Troutt and the Guppies. Jim Inman was the first bass player. He was a great student. His family was dedicated to real public service. He was the president of my senior class. He was one of the most compassionate humans I've ever known and still is. We played for a benefit once for some parents and kids with serious disabilities. It was time to go on stage and I couldn't find Jim. I looked out in the crowd and he was sitting on a blanket with a mother and horribly disfigured child.

I'll always remember the look on his face. There was no repulsion or pity just pure love coming out of his eyes. Again, a wonderful guy with a great family.

The comfort level was better without the age difference and jealously. We didn't have to start the learning process from scratch. We had a drummer trained from childhood with real showbusiness parents.

Both Steve and his sister Shelly were well-trained tap dancers and forced to take lessons since birth.

The Grimes family were showbusiness eccentric, and

Steve was an entertainer on and off stage.

Steve's parents, Marge and Jim Grimes, owned the costume shop in Indianapolis.

I learned a lot from our backstage father and mother and what it takes to produce a good show from behind the scenes.

Steve's dad Jim played sax before he went to war. A hand grenade was tossed into his transport truck and shrapnel ended his musical career. He was no lover of war or government.

Steve decided to introduce himself to me and the rest of Belzer Junior High in the lunch hall. The first time I ever saw him he climbed onto the lunch table and started tap dancing through everyone's food trays. He did not let the flying food or screaming fans distract him.

The assistant principal Bobbie Thiel (the pedophile) was waiting at the end of the table. Bobbie pulled Steve down by his arm and spanked his ass with his bare hand in front of everyone.

Steve and I have been friends for life even though he still tap dances in my lunch occasionally.

After some struggles with my injured ego and Marge we changed the band's name.

Marge had handmade these fake fur vests and covered Steve's drums in matching fuzz. She wanted to call the band the "Flintstones" (TV Cartoon from 1960-1966.)

Ironically, I chose the Fugitives (named after a TV series 1963-1967).

The Fugitives were getting good. Marge booked us to play a Batman theme show with costumed background batgirl dancers at the Indiana State Fair in 1966 (the Batman TV series came out in January of 1966).

Marge and I had the last-minute fall out after I noticed she had changed the Fugitives bass drumhead to "*STEVE GRIMES and the fugitives*".

We played that show without a bass drumhead and discovered the bass drum projected further without the drumhead. I'm not taking credit, but this did become a rock and roll trend.

The Grimes family were very good to me. They taught me that one monkey or organ grinder don't stop a show, the evils of jealously and other important rules of the street and stage.

But the greatest rule in show business or life is: **THE SHOW MUST GO ON.**

I was the student and I love them all to this very day. I will forever appreciate their time, patience, and forgiveness for my arrogant ways.

I played a snow-white Gibson Les Paul SG at the Indiana State Fair show. That was a guitar I loved and still think about like exotic women from the past.

In later years I got to talk to Les Paul at length at Willie Nelson's studio in Pedernales, Texas. Les was recording with

Willie and Bruce Hornsby and it was very laid back and casual as usual.

I got to ask Les Paul every question I had since I did my first sound on sound recording in Phil Ray's basement.

Les Paul sued Gibson over putting his name on the Gibson SG without his permission.

He was funny and he was young and I was thrilled to be in his unpretentious presence.

Bucky Meadows was a good friend and neighbor when I lived at Pedernales. We spent a lot of mornings drinking coffee, smoking pot and playing Cherokee guitar.

Bucky was Nashville's best and toured with Les Paul and Mary Ford when he was a child as the Gibson Child Prodigy.

Bucky is playing my old 1947 Epiphone Triumph at my house in Pedernales Country Club, Spicewood, Texas 1993

Bucky was naturally wired. The only time he wasn't pacing the floor he was playing. Rest in peace.

Let me back up.

CHAPTER NINETEEN—BLACK BOY IN THE BAND

GEORGE BENN WAS a magnificent singer. His father was the minister for the largest and most prosperous black church in Indianapolis. They had a beautiful home and drove a new "Duce and a Quarter" or what white people called a Buick Electra 225 back then.

George went on to do a great deal for music in Indianapolis and like my other friends he had a strong family background and support system.

George was not the James Brown stereotype, but he drove white women out of their minds. This is another phenomenon I'll address or undress later in one of my stories about race and sex.

The name of this band was the Indianapolis Soul Train. We were the first racially mixed band in Indianapolis.

George's family was one of the first black family I ever knew. He was the first black kid that ever spent the night at my house.

As the reality of Vietnam and government protests evolved, George became involved in the Black Power movement. By the time I left Indianapolis. George and I were both in protest costume and script.

You could feel an unwelcome wind developing. The dim lit alleys intrepid white kids had once traveled became darker and dangerous. There was a divide between the old school rules and the new school demand for social justice and equality.

This was a world dividing and then colliding. Our common struggles for racial equality and justice seemed to get hijacked, distorted and fought over by extremists.

CHAPTER TWENTY—CHUCK THE PIMP

HATRED SELLS, BUT it's hard to hate a guitar player. I found acceptance and appreciation on the other side of Indianapolis playing guitar in black jazz clubs. I led a double life, maybe even a triple life.

This started before I was old enough to legally drive or drink. The Hubbub, the 19th Hole, and the Hullabaloo were watering holes that did not check IDs close or care what color your skin was.

I was the kid in school that the cowardly kids asked to run the black liquor store gauntlet for half pints of Cherry, Orange, or Grape flavored vodka. You had to be light of foot and courageous to take on this assignment on a Friday night.

It would be fair to say I was a little ahead of my time and reasonably fearless. This started a pattern of meeting and making friends with other fearless gauntlet runners.

My first marijuana purchase came from a pimp named Chuck Humble in Indianapolis when I was 15. My parents would let me drive my first car to band practice before I got my license.

We were in front of Pearl's Whorehouse on 22nd and Delaware when we met. He was standing with 2 beautiful young women in prom dresses. I was driving a big black 1950 Dodge Coronet. It was a combination of an American Rolls Royce, a road grader, and a cheap hotel room with 2 cigarette lighters, one on each side of the back seat.

A Jimmy Pipe o' Peace

PRINCE ALBERT
the national joy smoke

has put the "Indian Sign" on all the tongue-broiling, smartweed brands. P. A. can't bite your tongue nor any man's, patented process removes the sting.

Sold everywhere in 5c bags, 10c tins, pound and half-pound humidors.

R. J. REYNOLDS TOBACCO CO.
Winston-Salem, N. C.

Chuck had never heard marijuana called grass before he met me. After bridging a language barrier, we settled on calling marijuana reefer.

This matchbox full of "reefer" cost $5.00. After consuming one matchbox of marijuana with the boys in the band, they handed me $5.00 each. I returned the next afternoon and told Chuck I needed 5 matchboxes of marijuana.

Chuck said, "No, you need a can. This was a metal Prince Albert tobacco can full of marijuana (21 matchboxes) for $20."

That paid for the grass, gas, and the prom dresses in later days.

Chuck and I fully understood the principals of multiplication. A lid of marijuana was a large jar lid of leveled off marijuana for about $10. A Folgers coffee can cost from $50 to $100.

This was before the mass production of marijuana and plastic bags. It takes approximately 5 pounds of plastic to wrap 100 pounds of marijuana for wholesale transport. Marijuana consumption turned the plastic bag industry into a multi-billion-dollar industry. Chuck and I should have bought stock in ZIP LOCK sandwich bags.

Chuck was a meticulous dresser and took at least 2 hours to get ready to hit the streets. The detail and time he took to primp and prep was amazing to watch. He was a showman of a different class. We became friends and I learned things from Chuck about human nature that you just won't find in a book.

CHAPTER TWENTY-ONE—MOZART TO MAHLER

INDIANAPOLIS HAD A classical music appreciation program in our public school system. This exposed many underprivileged kids to wonderful concerts and operas at Clowes Hall. These events would have been unaffordable and out of reach for most kids in public schools. I still deeply appreciate Opera, Mozart, Beethoven, Mahler and More. This music added a quality to my life that could never be taken from me. Chuck loved classical music.

Intelligence, Kindness and Generosity does trickle down. There was a close bond between the people that loved music in Indianapolis. Music transcended class and race and blurs the lines that divide us.

I could ride my bike to Wes Montgomery's house on Capitol Ave. He was my jazz guitar idol. I wore out 3 "Day in the Life" albums learning his style of playing octaves on the guitar with his thumb.

My music and friends came from all walks of religion and life. Indianapolis was a musical melting pot of Jews, Catholics, reasonably normal Protestants and Southern Missionary Baptists.

I was a Southern Missionary Baptist that accepted my mission, but I was never totally accepted by my church. But even Guyana Jim Jones got his start in Indianapolis.

CHAPTER TWENTY-TWO—LAST CALL FOR VIETNAM

THIS LAST BAND before Vietnam had evolved into the music I love the most, James Brown and the Fabulous Flames. And I got a chance to play the sax.

Today people don't remember the black and white only drinking fountains and the extreme rules of racial prejudice we lived under. I could not sit with my black friends at the back of the bus because I was white. You segregated or you walked.

Nonunion musicians could not perform at union dance halls and music venues in the 1960's. Blacks could not play in white clubs. My band could not play for the DeMolay dance at the Masonic Lodge in Lawrence, Indiana because we had a

Catholic drummer (Joe Holland).

My own grandmother cried her eyes out when I told her my 7th grade girlfriend was Catholic. I didn't know anything about girls or Catholics. I've been married to one for 40 years and still don't.

It's a mistake to ignore or underestimate this war for basic human rights versus our instinct to exploit weakness. Our ability to love each other and overcome this instinct is what makes us human.

Human accomplishment is a result of cooperation not competition. Music and marriage are the best examples. A good musician doesn't want or need to be the leader of the band, just an important part of the show.

Whether you're a musician or a mother the goal is: The Show Must Go On.

CHAPTER TWENTY-THREE—THE VOICES IN MY HEAD

A FEW FRIENDS stand out in my mind that put honesty, music, and justice for all before all else. The boys I left behind on the last call for Vietnam hurt the most.

Bob Halcomb and I were inseparable friends.

His parent's basement is where the heavy music and drug experimentation went down. We took long "Fear and Loathing" trips but never made it to Las Vegas.

We were cultivating cannabis in my parent's back yard, trading tabs of acid for grams of hash to our soldier friends in Germany, smoking weed smuggled from Jamaica in speakers and dropping LSD from the west coast long before we moved out of our parents' houses.

In fact, we drove them crazy.

Top row: Bob Halcomb, Richard Heilbrunn, Clyde Lieberman, Tom Embach and Rick Turney

Bob found an envelope of missing Red, White and Blue LSD (U.S. Military Grade) hidden in his mom's closet. She hijacked the acid Dickey Dickerson sent us from the U.S. mail. Tampering with the mail is a federal crime and she was lucky we didn't report her. But she was a loving mom and wonderful human being. God love and rest her soul.

Bob's parents left for the weekend, and we got high on the acid.

Bob was playing Rick's, new set of Slingerland drums from Santa Claus I believe. The bass drum vibrated too close to a space heater and that champagne pearl finish exploded like an oil refinery. But remember we're tripping on acid.

We tried to beat the fire out with my new collarless, powder blue blazer (sport jacket) and an iron skillet. Acid is not the best drug for emergencies.

We finally had to give up, flush the dope and call the fire department. Please don't think this was an isolated incident. This was just another Friday night.

We drove to Indiana Beach many times to see the Vanilla Fudge with Tim Bogart and Cactus. Carmine Appice played in both bands and was one of the world's greatest chemical rock drummers.

We went to the Atlanta Pop Festival with enough psychedelics to enlighten every catfish in the state of Georgia.

We took the deep, heavy, and far away trips together and made it back somehow.

Bob was also fast and physically powerful. He reacted to aggressive behavior with a surprising knockout punch. This happened faster than a cowboy can draw a gun. That skill and just that knowledge was reassuring. Bob gave me the courage to journey into some of the dimer lit alleys of exploration in our youth.

We lived on music and beginner's luck and should have died a thousand times. We almost froze to death driving to Naples, Florida in an old Austin Healy with no top and no heater. The very thought of the excitement wakes the wild side of me. Sometimes memories can create a brief longing for the past before the glamor fades to reality.

Bob had a fine-tuned ear for music. He dug up and spoon fed me the greatest music of our era. He had a lot of influence on the music I love now and play today. Bob was a teacher, a fighter and a musician's musician. We dropped a lot of acid, smoked a lot of dope. We did a lot of drinking and thinking about things you don't remember in the morning.

But there was never a dull moment and I have never regretted a minute. Those were the good ole days and our souls are fused together for all eternity. Two days after I finished this chapter Bob passed away. God bless and rest your soul dear brother).

Tom Embach was my girlfriend's younger brother. He was handsome, highly intelligent and played a great game of chess. He was a soldier in a war to end war. I had known him since he was a young boy and loved him like a brother. He wanted to put his foot in every stupid step I made in my pursuit of happiness, fame, and fortune.

Music is used and misused to lend credibility to words, actions, and people. Musicians of the Drug Rock era were unwitting Pied Pipers that glamorized alcoholism, drug abuse and casual sex, and lured many innocent kids into a glorified orgy of self-destruction.

Like Tommy and my sister, a lot of my friends and family put me on a pedestal and died emulating my behavior.

Tommy was introduced to the fast lane at an early age. He was killed in a high-speed chase with Marion County

Sheriff deputies over a half ounce baggie of marijuana. I think about him often, still miss his chess game and wonder what he might have become if that stop sign had not cut his head off.

I wonder how he would have lived had he never known or looked up to me.

Tommy's sister Kris was an excellent student, gymnast and preparing for college before she got pregnant and we got busted. I drugged and drug her through hell, ruined her reputation, wrecked her car, drove her crazy and dumped her when she needed me most. You can put me on a pedestal if you want, but I can't.

Rich Turney was the last drummer in my life before "last call for Vietnam". Rick came to Phoenix and stayed with me in an outlaw hideout close to 7th and Thunderbird for a while.

Rick was a health nut and would get up early every morning and run to the top of the little mountain by my house in the hot summer. Good drummers do weird things.

He would come back and shower with Dr. Bronner's peppermint soap until he shampooed away his hair.

One unusually hot and dry morning on Rick's return we smoked some of Richard's Afghan hash. Rick was hit with an uncontrollable hunger. He ate a large bag of granola by himself before he chugged two glasses of ice water. We thought his stomach was going to explode but he refused to go to the hospital. He looked like he was giving birth to a space alien. There should have been a petroglyph or warning on the granola bag about mixing health food, hashish and water.

Rick had a heart of gold and he was smart enough to tell

when things were going too far south.

I've always been grateful that Rick was smart enough to leave. Why are guys like Rick strong enough to avoid getting sucked down the vortex that has destroyed so many dreams and lives? Rick was another friend that had two parents and a strong family. I still think about how decent and kind they were to me.

Clyde Lieberman was a good friend and had a lot to do with getting the new music and message of peace and love out in Indianapolis. He was always at practice and pushing us forward. He knew more about music than any of us but worshipped the Grateful Dead for some unknown reason to me.

He would not hesitate to stand up to racial insensitivity or bullying even then. He wasn't a tough guy or a fighter, he just loved music and hated bullies.

CHAPTER TWENTY-FOUR—
JUNIOR'S FARM

AFTER I TURNED 19, I earned my diploma and draft notice at the same time. Somehow, I had managed to piss off Dan Quayle's grandfather (Eugene Pullium). Eugene Pullium was the owner and publisher of most of the Republican newspapers in the United States, like the Indianapolis Star News.

When I rented the big farmhouse with party barns and peaceful paisley pastures in Lebanon, Indiana I did not know that Eugene was my neighbor.

I did not know anything about Vice President Dan Quayle then. But I did know about Bret Kimberlin.[2]

---

[2] https://en.wikipedia.org/wiki/Brett_Kimberlin

Bob and I had a wall of Gibson and Fender amps stacked in the living room.

The jam sessions would go on for days and the party never stopped, it just kept getting bigger. We slept and partied in shifts.

The music was blasting, and the girls were making big pots of vegetable soup in the kitchen for the starving rich kids. They had all ran away from home to tune in, turn on and drop out at Junior's Farm in Lebanon, Indiana.

The boys were storing big bags of wild home-grown pot in the barn when 130 squad cars from different policing agencies arrived under a full moon. The musician's union may have been the only cops not represented and complaining.

The farm and music were an unsegregated island in a segregated sea of white foam. This is where the inner city met the suburbs.

The Electra 225 Buicks were in the long driveway when the cops arrived.

This is where the chocolate shake gets thick. Terry Masters was a close friend and had graduated with the older boys in the band. He landed a job at Dow Chemical. Terry started showing up with bags of white powder every couple of weeks. He said his job was to mix this powder in these large vats of distilled water to make what he called a "7% solution" for Eli Lily's cough syrup.

I didn't know anything about narcotics or that Dan Quayle's other grandfather owned Eli Lilly, the largest drug company in the world. The coincidence's started taking on a life of their own.

I did know the powder Terry had was incredibly powerful. My new rich friends from the inner city wanted that stuff more than their money, gold chains and girlfriends. I saw the raw powers that narcotics held over men and women. It was the most powerful force on earth. More powerful than love or money.

The party at Junior's farm was over and the police had a problem. The names on the guest list they collected were more than just embarrassing and did not make Eugene's newspapers. Eli Lilly did not make the news either.

Eugene asked the state of Indiana to give me the death penalty in his editorial about the evils of LSD and marijuana while Eli Lilly had the black community hooked on cough syrup.

CHAPTER TWENTY-FIVE—RUN FOR YOUR LIFE

BOB AND I were outside by the barn when the cops rolled in. We got away under a full moon across dimly lit fields, briars, barbed wire fences and a herd of pissed off horses. We could hear the dogs barking behind us as we moved down the tree lines to stay out of the moonlight.

All I could think about was how I was going to get my girlfriend and Les Paul out of that farmhouse.

We arrived at Richard Heilbrunn's farm at about daylight scratched up and exhausted.

We were in bad need of a joint, a beer, a place to hide out for a few days and a hug. Richard, his brother Paul, John

Jenkins, and Jerry Fitzgerald were hanging out there. They were close friends and well trusted members of an extended family and small underground community. We were bonded together by our commitment to end war, promote peace, love and enlightenment through the wholesale distribution of cannabis.

Richard Heilbrunn was the most spiritual among us and still is. Richard was as close to a holy man as you could find around Indianapolis in 1969 or around the world today.

There was no one more loved and respected in our family. John, Jerry and Richard seemed to love each other like brothers when I moved to Arizona.

But there was a falling out and John killed, Jerry, shot Richard 4 times and left him for dead. John drove to Canada, was arrested and hung himself in a Canadian jail.

These shots were heard around the world we lived in. I flew back from Arizona and visited Richard and his mom in the hospital.

As bad as Richard was hurt, I felt worse for his mother sitting by his side. My memories of Linda are a blessing to this day. God rest her soul.

This was at a time when doctors were passing out Thorazine like candy. It was getting used in our circle to come down off bad acid trips but Thorazine and acid are unpredictable and dangerous drugs. I could not think of any other explanation for what John did. LSD is a marvelous modern mental health medication, but it should be used in a controlled environment with competent supervision.

This story: the Yogurt Connection gives a fairly accurate account of what happened, but I'll never understand why it happened.[3]

According to People Magazine, Richard, his younger brother Paul and their mother Linda went on to become the *Masters of Deception*, "the biggest alleged marijuana smuggling operation ever encountered by the U.S. Government."[4]

Richard and his mother were not con artists out for the money, or murderers. They were out to make the world a better place.

Richard's brother Paul was handsome, well dressed and drove expensive cars. We had a falling out over some missing Mexican marijuana and did not speak for years. I'll save those stories for another book. However, I do not believe he has ever intentionally hurt anyone physically in his life.

Richard Heilbrunn still struggles with his injuries and probably the memories of that day. But Richard has preached nonviolence all the days I've known him. He has been the gold standard of peaceful political activism since we were teenagers. No one paid a higher price or got a worse deal than Richard, and his mother Linda for what they believed in.

---

[3] https://en.wikipedia.org/wiki/The_Yogurt_Connection
[4] https://people.com/archive/masters-of-deception-vol-31-no-24/

CHAPTER TWENTY-SIX—CHASING THE SUNSET

THE FIRST DRIVE from Indiana to Arizona in 1969 was a game changer. Driving through Salt River Canyon, and across the one lane bridges from Globe to Apache Junction was different than anything I had seen. Everything was much bigger and deeper than I could have imagined. This journey expanded my mind and exaggerated my horizons.

My road trip turned out to be a failed attempt to buy Mexican marijuana in Phoenix. I came back empty handed, but I felt more excitement than disappointment.

I packed my pregnant ole lady (afraid of heights), our flagellant basset hound named Doobie and my 1959 Les Paul in a 1964 Ford Fairlane and we hit the road.

Route 66 was in the process of dissolving into history with the completion of the East to West Coast Interstate system. These high-speed roadways between the two oceans were golden corridors of adventure, opportunity, and fortune.

CHAPTER TWENTY-SEVEN—GOLD CANYON GLITTERS

GOLD CANYON DID not exist when I passed the old Kings Ranch turn off on the way to Phoenix. I had no idea I would be tied to the end of that trail for the next 50 years.

At first, there was no one to hear or see me on Kings Ranch Ridge—though I could hear and see everything for miles. This mountain still gives me the sweetest water I've ever drank, showered with, or used to flush a toilet.

The old hunting trails and the road to the ranch faded into the desert as Gold Canyon began its evolution. Today it's difficult to imagine outlaw stories in this congested community of tract housing surrounded by extravagant luxury homes on the hills.

There are two resorts with golf courses sitting in this volatile canyon. Why would anyone cram themselves into the bottom of a dry canyon that floods in biblical proportion every 30 years or so?

We've had 3 one-hundred-year floods since 1970. The last big Arizona flood was in 1993. The urban sprawl of Gold Canyon came after the great floods. There has been nothing like these floods since that time.

Fifty years on this ridge reminds me of a movie I saw as a kid in 1960: *The Time Machine* starring Rod Taylor. A wealthy scientist built a machine that would take him into the future and past.

When he pushed the lever forward his house and the world around him evolved and dissolved along with civilization. As he accelerated into our future he saw the overpopulation, drought, flood, famine and war.

I saw the link between the destruction of the future and failures of our past.

Did this movie have as much impact on the other 10-year-old kids that saw it?

We risk losing our future when we forget our past. This motivates me to tell the stories that were buried with the broken pots in Gold Canyon.

The stars in the sky have been replaced by the glitter of twinkling lights across the desert. The night's silence has been drowned by the hum of air conditioners and air traffic over the mountains.

The robbed burial grounds have been sprinkled with fool's gold and Gold Canyon glitters like pyrite in the sun.

Indianapolis was left behind in a smoky cloud of legal, political, and moral chaos. Much happened in that fast and foggy period of life. Every mile took me further from my troubled past and into the unknown future of a fugitive.

I came to the Superstition Mountains to hide my family from my past. I needed a quiet, safe peaceful place to rest. That peace and safety I found did not last long.

What's important to this story and the ones to follow is I made it to Arizona with a pregnant ole lady, a guitar and a pack of hunting dogs on my ass.

These were turbulent times in my life. And to make a long story short: This is where Arlin Troutt found the entrance to the underworld and disappeared into the Superstition Mountains.

Arlin Troutt

THE END